INTERNATIONAL

Science Foundation

Activity Book A

Published by Collins
An imprint of HarperCollins*Publishers*
The News Building, 1 London Bridge Street,
London, SE1 9GF, UK

HarperCollins Publishers
Macken House, 39/40 Mayor Street Upper,
Dublin 1, D01 C9W8, Ireland

Browse the complete Collins catalogue at
www.collins.co.uk

© HarperCollins*Publishers* Limited 2021

10 9 8 7 6 5 4

ISBN 978-0-00-846870-5

British Library Cataloguing-in-Publication Data
A catalogue record for this publication is available from the British Library.

Author: Fiona Macgregor
Publisher: Elaine Higgleton
Product manager: Letitia Luff
Commissioning editor: Rachel Houghton
Edited by: Eleanor Barber
Editorial management: Oriel Square
Cover designer: Kevin Robbins
Cover illustrations: Jouve India Pvt Ltd.
Internal illustrations: Jouve India Pvt. Ltd.;
p 22c2 Laszlo Veres
Typesetter: Jouve India Pvt. Ltd.
Production controller: Lyndsey Rogers
Printed in India by Multivista Global Pvt. Ltd.

Acknowledgements

With thanks to all the kindergarten staff and their schools around the world who have helped with the development of this course, by sharing insights and commenting on and testing sample materials:

Calcutta International School: Sharmila Majumdar, Mrs Pratima Nayar, Preeti Roychoudhury, Tinku Yadav, Lakshmi Khanna, Mousumi Guha, Radhika Dhanuka, Archana Tiwari, Urmita Das; Gateway College (Sri Lanka): Kousala Benedict; Hawar International School: Kareen Barakat, Shahla Mohammed, Jennah Hussain; Manthan International School: Shalini Reddy; Monterey Pre-Primary: Adina Oram; Prometheus School: Aneesha Sahni, Deepa Nanda; Pragyanam School: Monika Sachdev; Rosary Sisters High School: Samar Sabat, Sireen Freij, Hiba Mousa; Solitaire Global School: Devi Nimmagadda; United Charter Schools (UCS): Tabassum Murtaza; Vietnam Australia International School: Holly Simpson

The publishers wish to thank the following for permission to reproduce photographs.

(t = top, c = centre, b = bottom, r = right, l = left)

p 9 Sergey Novikov/Shutterstock, p 15tl yevgeniy11/Shutterstock, p 15tr Osetrik/Shutterstock, p 15bl 5 second Studio/Shutterstock, p 15br Eric Isselee/Shutterstock, p 16tl Noheaphotos/Shutterstock, p 16tr Microfile.org/Shutterstock, p 16bl Meet Poddar/Shutterstock, p 16br Worraket/Shutterstock, p 22t Monkey Business Images/Shutterstock, p 22c1 AJP/Shutterstock, p 22b Kanea/Shutterstock

The publishers gratefully acknowledge the permission granted to reproduce the copyright material in this book. Every effort has been made to trace copyright holders and to obtain their permission for the use of copyright material. The publishers will gladly receive any information enabling them to rectify any error or omission at the first opportunity.

Extracts from Collins Big Cat readers reprinted by permission of HarperCollins *Publishers* Ltd

All © HarperCollins*Publishers*

MIX
Paper | Supporting
responsible forestry
FSC™ C007454

This book contains FSC™ certified paper and other controlled sources to ensure responsible forest management.

For more information visit: www.harpercollins.co.uk/green

Find

Find the items in the picture.
Draw a line from the item to the picture.

Date:

Circle

Circle the ones that are the same.
Use the same colour.

Date:

Match

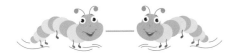

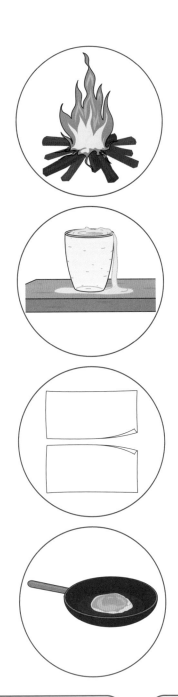

Say what will happen next. Match a picture
on the left with the correct picture on the right.   Date:

Draw

Draw the things you saw on your nature walk.

Date:

Cross

Put a cross next to the non-living things.

Date:

Sort

Living things	Non-living things

PCM 1. Cut up the pictures. Stick the living things in the green box. Stick the non-living things in the blue box.   Date:

Trace and say

I move.

I breathe.

I grow.

I eat.

Trace around the pictures. Say the sentences.

Date:

Match

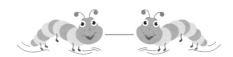

head

neck

arm

stomach

hand

leg

foot

Match the parts of the body to the boy.

Date:

Match

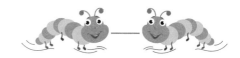

Match the senses to the pictures.

Date:

Find and colour

1

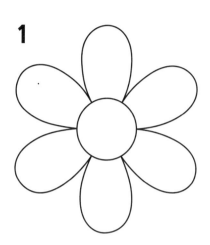
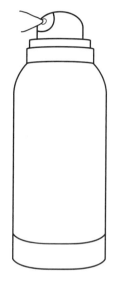

2

1 Colour in the things that smell nice.
2 Colour in the things that taste nice.

Date:

Circle

Circle the things that feel hard.

Date:

Draw

Draw the things you can hear right now.

Date:

Trace and say

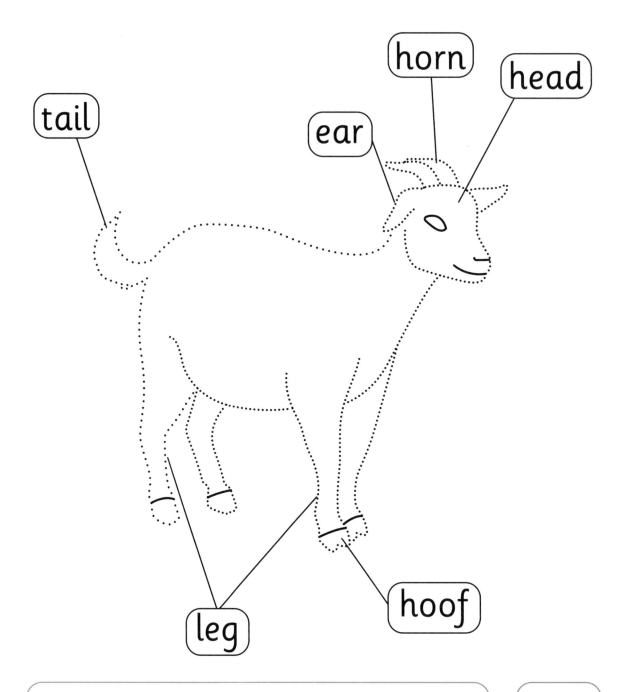

Trace around the goat. Say the words.

Date:

Look and say

goat

horse

cat

rabbit

Look at the pictures. What is the same about these animals?	Date:	

Look and say

fish

butterfly

tortoise

snake

Look at the pictures.
What is different about these animals?   Date:

Draw

Draw your favourite animal.

Date:

Cut and stick

PCM 5. Cut out the pieces.
Stick them in the correct place on the plant.   Date:

Match

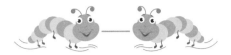

Draw a line to match the flowers with the same shape.

Date:

Find and circle

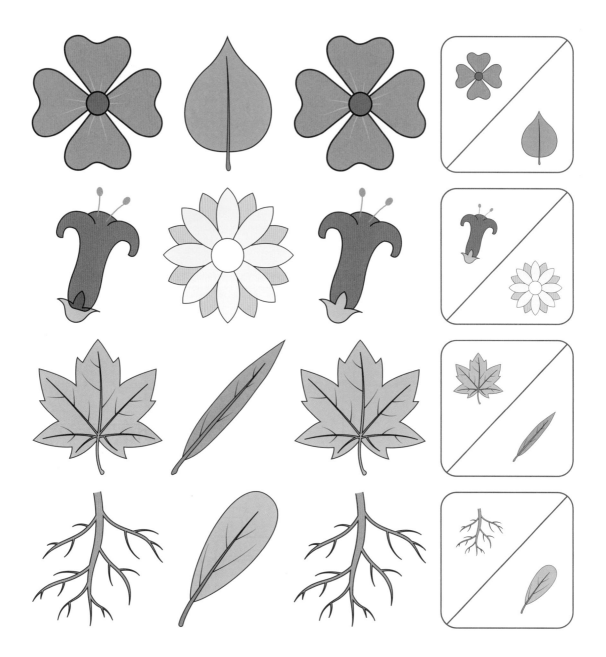

Follow the pattern in each line.
Circle what comes next.

Date:

Draw

Draw the plant that you are growing.

Date:

Match

We are living
things.

Which animals
are the same?

I use my senses.

Plants are living
things too.

Match the sentences to the pictures.

Date:

Review

Tick

☐ I can find.

☐ I can match.

☐ I can draw.

☐ I can sort.

☐ I can trace and say.

☐ I can find and colour.

☐ I can circle.

☐ I can look and say.

☐ I can cut and stick.

Tick what you can do.

Date:

Assessment record

_____ has achieved these Science Foundation Phase Objectives:

Use scientific enquiry skills (ask, predict, sort, demonstrate)	1	2	3
Explain the difference between living and non-living things	1	2	3
Know some characteristics of living things	1	2	3
Describe the basic external structure of the human body	1	2	3
Identify different sense organs	1	2	3
Describe how we use our sense organs in everyday life	1	2	3
Identify and name some common animals	1	2	3
Know the basic external structure of some common animals	1	2	3
Know that animals are living things	1	2	3
Identify different plants in their local environment	1	2	3
Know that plants are living things	1	2	3
Know the basic parts of a plant	1	2	3
Recognise that there is a variety of different leaves and flowers	1	2	3

1: Partially achieved
2: Achieved
3: Exceeded

Signed by teacher:
Signed by parent: Date: